50 Bread Lover's Guide Recipes

By: Kelly Johnson

Table of Contents

- Classic Sourdough Bread
- French Baguette
- Focaccia with Rosemary and Sea Salt
- Whole Wheat Bread
- Brioche Loaf
- Cinnamon Swirl Bread
- Challah
- Ciabatta Bread
- Potato Bread
- Irish Soda Bread
- Multigrain Bread
- Naan
- Fougasse with Olives and Herbs
- Pita Bread
- Pull-Apart Garlic Bread
- Olive Bread
- Rye Bread
- Panettone
- Flatbread with Za'atar
- Seeded Sourdough
- Soft Dinner Rolls
- English Muffins
- Pretzels
- Bagels
- Sweet Cornbread
- Pane di Altamura
- French Pain de Campagne
- Turkish Simit
- Beer Bread
- Spelt Bread
- White Sandwich Bread
- Anadama Bread
- Milk Bread
- Lavash
- Gluten-Free Bread

- Italian Semolina Bread
- Tuscan Bread
- Honey Whole Wheat Bread
- Rustic Country Bread
- Sweet Potato Bread
- Croissants
- Brioche Buns
- Pumpernickel Bread
- Garlic Herb Breadsticks
- Chia Seed Bread
- Focaccia with Cherry Tomatoes and Basil
- Mediterranean Olive and Herb Loaf
- Cornmeal Bread
- Pretzel Buns
- Scandinavian Rye Bread

Classic Sourdough Bread

Ingredients:

- 500g bread flour
- 375ml water
- 100g active sourdough starter
- 10g salt

Instructions:

1. In a large bowl, mix flour, water, and sourdough starter. Let rest for 30 minutes.
2. Add salt and knead for 8-10 minutes until smooth.
3. Let the dough rise in a covered bowl for 4-6 hours, or until doubled in size.
4. Shape the dough into a round loaf, and let it rise for another 1-2 hours.
5. Preheat the oven to 230°C (450°F). Bake for 30-40 minutes until the bread has a golden, crispy crust.

French Baguette

Ingredients:

- 500g bread flour
- 350ml water
- 10g salt
- 10g instant yeast

Instructions:

1. Mix flour, water, salt, and yeast into a dough. Knead for 10 minutes until smooth.
2. Let the dough rise for 1-2 hours or until doubled.
3. Shape the dough into long baguettes and let them rise for 1 hour.
4. Preheat the oven to 220°C (425°F). Make slashes on the baguettes and bake for 20-25 minutes until golden brown.

Focaccia with Rosemary and Sea Salt

Ingredients:

- 500g all-purpose flour
- 300ml water
- 10g salt
- 2 tbsp olive oil
- 10g active dry yeast
- 1 tbsp fresh rosemary, chopped
- Coarse sea salt

Instructions:

1. Combine flour, yeast, and salt in a bowl. Gradually add water and knead for 8-10 minutes.
2. Let the dough rise for 1-2 hours until doubled.
3. Preheat the oven to 200°C (400°F). Roll the dough into a thick rectangle and transfer it to a baking sheet.
4. Drizzle with olive oil, sprinkle with rosemary and sea salt, and bake for 20-25 minutes until golden brown.

Whole Wheat Bread

Ingredients:

- 500g whole wheat flour
- 300ml water
- 10g salt
- 7g dry yeast
- 2 tbsp olive oil

Instructions:

1. Combine all ingredients into a dough and knead for 8-10 minutes.
2. Let the dough rise for 1 hour or until doubled in size.
3. Shape into a loaf and place it in a greased bread pan. Let it rise for another hour.
4. Preheat the oven to 180°C (350°F) and bake for 30-40 minutes.

Brioche Loaf

Ingredients:

- 500g all-purpose flour
- 100g butter, softened
- 250ml milk
- 50g sugar
- 10g salt
- 20g fresh yeast
- 4 eggs

Instructions:

1. Mix flour, sugar, salt, and yeast. Add eggs and milk, and knead until smooth.
2. Gradually add butter and knead until fully incorporated.
3. Let the dough rise for 1-2 hours until doubled.
4. Preheat the oven to 180°C (350°F). Shape dough into a loaf, place it in a greased pan, and let it rise for 1 hour.
5. Bake for 25-30 minutes until golden brown.

Cinnamon Swirl Bread

Ingredients:

- 500g bread flour
- 250ml milk
- 100g butter
- 100g sugar
- 2 tsp ground cinnamon
- 10g instant yeast
- 1 egg
- 1 tsp vanilla extract

Instructions:

1. Mix flour, yeast, sugar, and cinnamon. Add milk, butter, egg, and vanilla, and knead until smooth.
2. Let the dough rise for 1-2 hours.
3. Roll the dough into a rectangle, sprinkle with cinnamon sugar, and roll it up tightly.
4. Preheat the oven to 180°C (350°F). Place in a greased pan, and bake for 30-40 minutes.

Challah

Ingredients:

- 500g bread flour
- 300ml warm water
- 50g sugar
- 10g salt
- 7g active dry yeast
- 2 eggs
- 100g butter, melted

Instructions:

1. Mix flour, sugar, salt, and yeast. Add water, eggs, and melted butter, and knead until smooth.
2. Let the dough rise for 1-2 hours.
3. Braid the dough into a challah shape, and let it rise for another hour.
4. Preheat the oven to 180°C (350°F) and bake for 30-35 minutes until golden.

Ciabatta Bread

Ingredients:

- 500g bread flour
- 400ml water
- 10g salt
- 10g active dry yeast
- 2 tbsp olive oil

Instructions:

1. Mix flour, yeast, and salt. Gradually add water and knead into a sticky dough.
2. Let the dough rise for 2 hours or until doubled.
3. Preheat the oven to 220°C (425°F). Shape the dough into a flat, rectangular shape and bake for 20-25 minutes.
4. Let the bread cool before slicing.

Potato Bread

Ingredients:

- 500g bread flour
- 300g mashed potatoes
- 7g instant yeast
- 250ml warm water
- 10g salt
- 2 tbsp olive oil

Instructions:

1. Combine flour, yeast, and salt. Add warm water, mashed potatoes, and olive oil.
2. Mix and knead for 8-10 minutes until smooth.
3. Let the dough rise for 1-2 hours until doubled.
4. Shape into a loaf and let it rise for 1 hour.
5. Preheat the oven to 200°C (400°F) and bake for 25-30 minutes until golden brown.

Irish Soda Bread

Ingredients:

- 450g all-purpose flour
- 1 tsp baking soda
- 10g salt
- 300ml buttermilk

Instructions:

1. Preheat the oven to 180°C (350°F).
2. In a bowl, mix flour, baking soda, and salt. Add buttermilk and stir to form a dough.
3. Knead briefly, then shape into a round loaf.
4. Score a deep cross on top of the dough.
5. Bake for 30-40 minutes until the bread sounds hollow when tapped.

Multigrain Bread

Ingredients:

- 300g whole wheat flour
- 200g all-purpose flour
- 100g mixed seeds (sunflower, flax, sesame)
- 10g salt
- 7g instant yeast
- 300ml warm water
- 2 tbsp honey

Instructions:

1. Mix flours, seeds, salt, and yeast in a bowl. Add warm water and honey.
2. Knead the dough for 8-10 minutes until smooth.
3. Let the dough rise for 1-2 hours.
4. Shape into a loaf, place in a greased pan, and let it rise for another hour.
5. Preheat the oven to 180°C (350°F) and bake for 30-40 minutes.

Naan

Ingredients:

- 500g all-purpose flour
- 7g instant yeast
- 10g salt
- 1 tsp sugar
- 250ml warm yogurt
- 50g melted butter

Instructions:

1. Combine flour, yeast, sugar, and salt in a bowl. Add yogurt and melted butter.
2. Knead the dough for 10 minutes, then let it rise for 1-2 hours.
3. Preheat a skillet or tandoor.
4. Divide the dough into small balls and roll them into flat discs.
5. Cook naan in the hot skillet for 2-3 minutes per side, brushing with more butter.

Fougasse with Olives and Herbs

Ingredients:

- 500g bread flour
- 10g salt
- 7g dry yeast
- 300ml water
- 2 tbsp olive oil
- 100g black olives, pitted and chopped
- 1 tbsp fresh rosemary, chopped

Instructions:

1. Combine flour, yeast, and salt in a bowl. Gradually add water and olive oil.
2. Knead until smooth, then let the dough rise for 1-2 hours.
3. Flatten the dough into a rectangle and scatter olives and rosemary on top.
4. Preheat the oven to 200°C (400°F). Bake for 20-25 minutes until golden and crispy.

Pita Bread

Ingredients:

- 500g all-purpose flour
- 10g salt
- 7g dry yeast
- 1 tbsp olive oil
- 300ml warm water

Instructions:

1. Mix flour, salt, and yeast in a bowl. Gradually add warm water and olive oil.
2. Knead the dough for 10 minutes.
3. Let the dough rise for 1-2 hours.
4. Preheat the oven to 250°C (475°F) and place a baking stone or sheet inside.
5. Divide the dough into small balls and roll them into flat discs.
6. Bake on the hot stone for 5-7 minutes until puffy and golden.

Pull-Apart Garlic Bread

Ingredients:

- 500g all-purpose flour
- 10g salt
- 7g dry yeast
- 300ml warm water
- 100g butter, melted
- 5 cloves garlic, minced
- Fresh parsley, chopped

Instructions:

1. Mix flour, yeast, and salt in a bowl. Gradually add warm water and knead for 10 minutes.
2. Let the dough rise for 1-2 hours.
3. Preheat the oven to 180°C (350°F).
4. Roll the dough into small balls and layer them in a greased pan.
5. Mix melted butter, garlic, and parsley, and pour over the dough.
6. Bake for 25-30 minutes until golden and crispy.

Olive Bread

Ingredients:

- 500g bread flour
- 10g salt
- 7g dry yeast
- 300ml warm water
- 100g green and black olives, chopped
- 2 tbsp olive oil

Instructions:

1. Combine flour, yeast, and salt in a bowl. Add warm water and olive oil.
2. Knead the dough for 10 minutes.
3. Add olives and knead until evenly distributed.
4. Let the dough rise for 1-2 hours.
5. Preheat the oven to 180°C (350°F). Shape the dough into a loaf and bake for 30-40 minutes until golden.

Rye Bread

Ingredients:

- 300g rye flour
- 200g bread flour
- 7g instant yeast
- 10g salt
- 1 tbsp caraway seeds (optional)
- 250ml warm water
- 1 tbsp honey

Instructions:

1. Combine rye flour, bread flour, yeast, salt, and caraway seeds (if using) in a bowl.
2. Gradually add warm water and honey, mixing until a dough forms.
3. Knead for 8-10 minutes until smooth.
4. Let the dough rise for 1-2 hours until doubled.
5. Shape the dough into a loaf, place it in a greased pan, and let it rise for another hour.
6. Preheat the oven to 200°C (400°F) and bake for 30-40 minutes until the bread sounds hollow when tapped.

Panettone

Ingredients:

- 500g bread flour
- 150g sugar
- 10g salt
- 7g instant yeast
- 5 large eggs
- 200ml milk
- 200g butter, softened
- 200g candied fruit
- 100g raisins
- 1 tbsp vanilla extract

Instructions:

1. Mix flour, sugar, salt, and yeast in a large bowl.
2. In a separate bowl, whisk eggs, milk, and vanilla. Add to dry ingredients and knead until smooth.
3. Gradually incorporate softened butter and knead for 10 minutes.
4. Let the dough rise for 1-2 hours, then fold in candied fruit and raisins.
5. Shape the dough into a round loaf and place it in a panettone mold.
6. Let it rise for another 2 hours. Preheat the oven to 175°C (350°F) and bake for 40-50 minutes.

Flatbread with Za'atar

Ingredients:

- 300g all-purpose flour
- 7g instant yeast
- 10g salt
- 1 tbsp olive oil
- 200ml warm water
- 2 tbsp za'atar spice blend
- 2 tbsp olive oil (for topping)

Instructions:

1. Combine flour, yeast, and salt in a bowl. Add warm water and olive oil, and mix into a dough.
2. Knead for 8-10 minutes until smooth.
3. Let the dough rise for 1 hour.
4. Preheat the oven to 220°C (425°F).
5. Roll out the dough into a flat, round shape. Drizzle with olive oil and sprinkle with za'atar.
6. Bake for 10-12 minutes until golden.

Seeded Sourdough

Ingredients:

- 500g bread flour
- 100g whole wheat flour
- 100g sourdough starter
- 10g salt
- 50g sunflower seeds
- 50g pumpkin seeds
- 300ml water

Instructions:

1. Mix both flours, sourdough starter, salt, and water in a large bowl.
2. Knead for 8-10 minutes, incorporating seeds halfway through.
3. Let the dough rise for 4-6 hours, or overnight in the fridge.
4. Shape the dough into a round loaf and let it rise for another 2 hours.
5. Preheat the oven to 230°C (450°F) and bake for 30-35 minutes until golden.

Soft Dinner Rolls

Ingredients:

- 500g all-purpose flour
- 7g instant yeast
- 10g salt
- 50g sugar
- 250ml warm milk
- 50g butter, melted
- 1 egg

Instructions:

1. Mix flour, yeast, salt, and sugar in a bowl. Add warm milk, melted butter, and egg.
2. Knead until smooth, then let the dough rise for 1 hour.
3. Divide the dough into small balls and place them in a greased pan.
4. Let the rolls rise for 30 minutes. Preheat the oven to 180°C (350°F).
5. Bake for 15-20 minutes until golden brown.

English Muffins

Ingredients:

- 500g all-purpose flour
- 7g instant yeast
- 10g salt
- 1 tbsp sugar
- 250ml warm milk
- 50g butter, melted
- Cornmeal for dusting

Instructions:

1. Mix flour, yeast, salt, and sugar in a bowl. Add warm milk and melted butter, then mix into a dough.
2. Knead for 8-10 minutes until smooth.
3. Let the dough rise for 1 hour.
4. Roll out the dough to 1 cm thick and cut into rounds.
5. Preheat a griddle or skillet and dust with cornmeal. Cook the muffins for 5-6 minutes per side until golden and cooked through.

Pretzels

Ingredients:

- 500g bread flour
- 7g instant yeast
- 10g salt
- 1 tbsp sugar
- 250ml warm water
- 50g baking soda (for boiling)
- Coarse sea salt

Instructions:

1. Mix flour, yeast, salt, sugar, and warm water into a dough.
2. Knead for 10 minutes until smooth.
3. Let the dough rise for 1-2 hours.
4. Preheat the oven to 220°C (425°F) and bring a pot of water to a boil with baking soda.
5. Shape the dough into pretzels, then boil them for 30 seconds each.
6. Place them on a baking sheet, sprinkle with coarse sea salt, and bake for 15-20 minutes until golden.

Bagels

Ingredients:

- 500g bread flour
- 7g instant yeast
- 10g salt
- 1 tbsp sugar
- 250ml warm water
- 2 tbsp honey (for boiling)
- Sesame seeds or poppy seeds (optional)

Instructions:

1. Mix flour, yeast, salt, sugar, and warm water into a dough.
2. Knead for 10 minutes, then let the dough rise for 1 hour.
3. Preheat the oven to 220°C (425°F) and bring a pot of water to a boil with honey.
4. Shape the dough into bagels and boil for 1-2 minutes on each side.
5. Sprinkle with seeds, then bake for 15-20 minutes until golden.

Sweet Cornbread

Ingredients:

- 250g cornmeal
- 200g all-purpose flour
- 10g baking powder
- 100g sugar
- 1/2 tsp salt
- 2 large eggs
- 250ml milk
- 100g butter, melted

Instructions:

1. Preheat the oven to 180°C (350°F). Grease a baking pan.
2. Mix cornmeal, flour, baking powder, sugar, and salt.
3. In a separate bowl, whisk eggs, milk, and melted butter.
4. Combine wet and dry ingredients and pour into the prepared pan.
5. Bake for 25-30 minutes until golden and a toothpick comes out clean.

Pane di Altamura

Ingredients:

- 500g semolina flour
- 300g bread flour
- 15g salt
- 7g instant yeast
- 400ml warm water
- 1 tbsp olive oil

Instructions:

1. Mix the semolina flour, bread flour, salt, and yeast in a large bowl.
2. Gradually add warm water and olive oil, mixing until a dough forms.
3. Knead for 10 minutes until smooth, then let the dough rise for 1-2 hours.
4. Shape the dough into a round loaf and place it on a floured surface.
5. Preheat the oven to 220°C (430°F) and bake for 35-40 minutes until golden and hollow when tapped.

French Pain de Campagne

Ingredients:

- 500g all-purpose flour
- 10g salt
- 7g instant yeast
- 350ml warm water
- 1 tbsp olive oil

Instructions:

1. In a bowl, combine flour, salt, and yeast. Gradually add water and olive oil.
2. Mix into a dough and knead for about 10 minutes until smooth.
3. Let the dough rise for 1-2 hours until doubled.
4. Shape the dough into a round or oval loaf, and let it rise again for about 30 minutes.
5. Preheat the oven to 220°C (425°F) and bake for 30-35 minutes until golden.

Turkish Simit

Ingredients:

- 500g all-purpose flour
- 10g salt
- 10g sugar
- 7g instant yeast
- 250ml warm water
- 1 tbsp olive oil
- 100g sesame seeds

Instructions:

1. Mix flour, salt, sugar, and yeast in a large bowl. Gradually add warm water and olive oil.
2. Knead the dough for 10 minutes, then let it rise for 1 hour.
3. Divide the dough into equal portions and roll each into a long rope.
4. Shape each rope into a circle, dipping them in water and then sesame seeds.
5. Preheat the oven to 200°C (400°F) and bake for 20-25 minutes until golden and crisp.

Beer Bread

Ingredients:

- 375g all-purpose flour
- 10g salt
- 15g sugar
- 7g instant yeast
- 330ml beer (preferably a lager or ale)
- 2 tbsp melted butter

Instructions:

1. Mix flour, salt, sugar, and yeast in a bowl.
2. Gradually add beer, stirring until a dough forms.
3. Transfer the dough to a greased loaf pan, and smooth the top.
4. Let it rise for about 30 minutes.
5. Preheat the oven to 180°C (350°F), brush the top with melted butter, and bake for 30-35 minutes until golden.

Spelt Bread

Ingredients:

- 500g spelt flour
- 10g salt
- 7g instant yeast
- 350ml warm water
- 1 tbsp olive oil

Instructions:

1. Combine spelt flour, salt, and yeast in a large bowl.
2. Add warm water and olive oil, and mix to form a dough.
3. Knead for 10 minutes until smooth and elastic.
4. Let the dough rise for 1-2 hours until doubled.
5. Shape the dough into a loaf, place it in a greased pan, and let it rise again for 30 minutes.
6. Preheat the oven to 200°C (400°F) and bake for 30-35 minutes until golden.

White Sandwich Bread

Ingredients:

- 500g all-purpose flour
- 10g salt
- 7g instant yeast
- 300ml warm water
- 30g sugar
- 30g butter, softened

Instructions:

1. Mix flour, salt, yeast, and sugar in a bowl.
2. Gradually add warm water and butter, mixing to form a dough.
3. Knead for 8-10 minutes until smooth.
4. Let the dough rise for 1 hour, then punch it down and shape it into a loaf.
5. Place in a greased loaf pan and let it rise for another hour.
6. Preheat the oven to 180°C (350°F) and bake for 25-30 minutes until golden.

Anadama Bread

Ingredients:

- 350g all-purpose flour
- 150g cornmeal
- 7g instant yeast
- 10g salt
- 300ml warm water
- 2 tbsp molasses
- 30g butter, softened

Instructions:

1. Combine flour, cornmeal, yeast, and salt in a bowl.
2. Add warm water, molasses, and butter, mixing to form a dough.
3. Knead for 10 minutes until smooth.
4. Let the dough rise for 1-2 hours until doubled.
5. Shape the dough into a loaf and place it in a greased pan. Let it rise for another 30 minutes.
6. Preheat the oven to 180°C (350°F) and bake for 30-35 minutes until golden.

Milk Bread

Ingredients:

- 500g all-purpose flour
- 10g salt
- 7g instant yeast
- 250ml warm milk
- 50g sugar
- 30g butter, softened

Instructions:

1. In a large bowl, mix flour, salt, yeast, and sugar.
2. Gradually add warm milk and softened butter, mixing to form a dough.
3. Knead for 10 minutes until smooth and elastic.
4. Let the dough rise for 1-2 hours, then shape it into a loaf.
5. Place the dough in a greased pan, cover, and let it rise for another 30 minutes.
6. Preheat the oven to 180°C (350°F) and bake for 30-35 minutes until golden.

Lavash

Ingredients:

- 500g all-purpose flour
- 10g salt
- 7g instant yeast
- 300ml warm water
- 1 tbsp olive oil
- 1 tsp sugar

Instructions:

1. Combine flour, salt, and yeast in a bowl.
2. Add warm water, olive oil, and sugar, then mix into a dough.
3. Knead for 8-10 minutes until smooth.
4. Let the dough rise in a warm place for 1 hour.
5. Preheat the oven to 220°C (430°F).
6. Divide the dough into small balls, then roll each into a thin circle.
7. Bake for 3-5 minutes on a baking sheet until slightly golden and crispy.

Gluten-Free Bread

Ingredients:

- 500g gluten-free flour blend
- 10g salt
- 7g instant yeast
- 350ml warm water
- 30g sugar
- 2 tbsp olive oil
- 1 tsp apple cider vinegar

Instructions:

1. Combine the gluten-free flour, salt, and yeast in a bowl.
2. Add warm water, sugar, olive oil, and apple cider vinegar. Stir to form a dough.
3. Let the dough rise for 1 hour in a warm place.
4. Transfer the dough to a greased loaf pan and smooth the top.
5. Preheat the oven to 180°C (350°F) and bake for 30-35 minutes until golden.

Italian Semolina Bread

Ingredients:

- 400g semolina flour
- 100g all-purpose flour
- 10g salt
- 7g instant yeast
- 350ml warm water
- 2 tbsp olive oil

Instructions:

1. In a bowl, mix semolina flour, all-purpose flour, salt, and yeast.
2. Gradually add warm water and olive oil, mixing into a dough.
3. Knead for 10 minutes until smooth.
4. Let the dough rise for 1-2 hours until doubled.
5. Shape the dough into a loaf and let it rise for 30 minutes.
6. Preheat the oven to 220°C (430°F) and bake for 30-35 minutes until golden.

Tuscan Bread

Ingredients:

- 500g all-purpose flour
- 10g salt
- 7g instant yeast
- 350ml warm water
- 1 tbsp olive oil

Instructions:

1. Mix the flour, salt, and yeast in a bowl.
2. Add warm water and olive oil, stirring to form a dough.
3. Knead for 8-10 minutes, then let the dough rise for 1 hour.
4. Shape the dough into a rustic loaf and let it rise again for 30 minutes.
5. Preheat the oven to 220°C (430°F).
6. Bake for 30-35 minutes until golden and hollow when tapped.

Honey Whole Wheat Bread

Ingredients:

- 300g whole wheat flour
- 200g all-purpose flour
- 10g salt
- 7g instant yeast
- 300ml warm water
- 2 tbsp honey
- 2 tbsp olive oil

Instructions:

1. Mix the whole wheat flour, all-purpose flour, salt, and yeast in a bowl.
2. Add warm water, honey, and olive oil, stirring to form a dough.
3. Knead for 8-10 minutes until smooth.
4. Let the dough rise for 1 hour.
5. Shape the dough into a loaf and let it rise for 30 minutes.
6. Preheat the oven to 180°C (350°F) and bake for 30-35 minutes until golden.

Rustic Country Bread

Ingredients:

- 500g all-purpose flour
- 10g salt
- 7g instant yeast
- 350ml warm water
- 1 tbsp olive oil

Instructions:

1. Combine the flour, salt, and yeast in a large bowl.
2. Add warm water and olive oil, mixing to form a dough.
3. Knead for 8-10 minutes until smooth.
4. Let the dough rise for 1-2 hours until doubled in size.
5. Shape the dough into a rustic round loaf and let it rise for 30 minutes.
6. Preheat the oven to 220°C (430°F) and bake for 30-35 minutes until golden and crusty.

Sweet Potato Bread

Ingredients:

- 500g all-purpose flour
- 10g salt
- 7g instant yeast
- 300g mashed sweet potato
- 300ml warm water
- 30g sugar
- 2 tbsp butter, softened

Instructions:

1. Mix the flour, salt, and yeast in a bowl.
2. Add mashed sweet potato, warm water, sugar, and butter, mixing into a dough.
3. Knead for 8-10 minutes until smooth.
4. Let the dough rise for 1 hour.
5. Shape the dough into a loaf and let it rise for another 30 minutes.
6. Preheat the oven to 180°C (350°F) and bake for 30-35 minutes until golden.

Croissants

Ingredients:

- 500g all-purpose flour
- 10g salt
- 50g sugar
- 20g instant yeast
- 250ml warm milk
- 300g cold butter, cubed
- 1 egg (for egg wash)

Instructions:

1. Combine flour, salt, sugar, and yeast in a bowl.
2. Add warm milk and mix into a dough. Knead for 10 minutes until smooth.
3. Let the dough rise for 1-2 hours, then refrigerate for 1 hour.
4. Roll the dough into a rectangle, place the cold butter in the center, and fold the dough over.
5. Roll out again, fold, and repeat this process two more times.
6. Roll the dough into a large rectangle and cut into triangles.
7. Roll each triangle from the base to the tip and place on a baking sheet.
8. Let the croissants rise for 1 hour.
9. Preheat the oven to 200°C (400°F), brush with egg wash, and bake for 15-20 minutes until golden and puffed.

Brioche Buns

Ingredients:

- 500g all-purpose flour
- 7g instant yeast
- 50g sugar
- 10g salt
- 3 large eggs
- 250ml milk
- 150g unsalted butter, softened
- 1 egg (for egg wash)

Instructions:

1. Mix flour, yeast, sugar, and salt in a large bowl.
2. Add eggs, milk, and butter, and mix until a dough forms.
3. Knead for 10 minutes until smooth.
4. Let the dough rise for 1-2 hours until doubled in size.
5. Shape the dough into buns and place on a baking sheet.
6. Let the buns rise for 30-45 minutes.
7. Preheat the oven to 180°C (350°F) and bake for 15-20 minutes.
8. Brush with egg wash before baking for a golden finish.

Pumpernickel Bread

Ingredients:

- 300g whole wheat flour
- 200g rye flour
- 10g salt
- 7g instant yeast
- 350ml warm water
- 2 tbsp molasses
- 1 tbsp caraway seeds

Instructions:

1. Combine whole wheat flour, rye flour, salt, and yeast in a bowl.
2. Add warm water, molasses, and caraway seeds, mixing to form a dough.
3. Knead for 8-10 minutes until smooth.
4. Let the dough rise for 1-2 hours.
5. Shape the dough into a loaf and place it on a greased baking pan.
6. Preheat the oven to 180°C (350°F) and bake for 35-40 minutes until golden.

Garlic Herb Breadsticks

Ingredients:

- 500g all-purpose flour
- 10g salt
- 7g instant yeast
- 300ml warm water
- 3 tbsp olive oil
- 4 cloves garlic, minced
- 1 tbsp mixed herbs (oregano, thyme, rosemary)

Instructions:

1. Combine flour, salt, and yeast in a bowl.
2. Add warm water and olive oil, mixing into a dough.
3. Knead for 8-10 minutes.
4. Let the dough rise for 1 hour.
5. Preheat the oven to 200°C (400°F).
6. Roll the dough into long sticks and place on a baking sheet.
7. Brush with olive oil, minced garlic, and herbs.
8. Bake for 12-15 minutes until golden and crisp.

Chia Seed Bread

Ingredients:

- 300g all-purpose flour
- 100g whole wheat flour
- 10g salt
- 7g instant yeast
- 350ml warm water
- 2 tbsp chia seeds
- 1 tbsp honey

Instructions:

1. Mix flours, salt, yeast, and chia seeds in a large bowl.
2. Add warm water and honey, mixing into a dough.
3. Knead for 8-10 minutes until smooth.
4. Let the dough rise for 1-2 hours.
5. Shape the dough into a loaf and let it rise for 30 minutes.
6. Preheat the oven to 180°C (350°F) and bake for 30-35 minutes.

Focaccia with Cherry Tomatoes and Basil

Ingredients:

- 500g all-purpose flour
- 7g instant yeast
- 10g salt
- 350ml warm water
- 3 tbsp olive oil
- 1 cup cherry tomatoes, halved
- Fresh basil leaves

Instructions:

1. Mix flour, yeast, and salt in a bowl.
2. Add warm water and olive oil, mixing to form a dough.
3. Knead for 8-10 minutes.
4. Let the dough rise for 1 hour.
5. Preheat the oven to 220°C (430°F).
6. Spread the dough onto a baking sheet and press in the cherry tomatoes and basil.
7. Drizzle with olive oil and bake for 20-25 minutes until golden.

Mediterranean Olive and Herb Loaf

Ingredients:

- 500g all-purpose flour
- 7g instant yeast
- 10g salt
- 350ml warm water
- 1/2 cup pitted olives, chopped
- 1 tbsp dried oregano
- 2 tbsp olive oil

Instructions:

1. Mix flour, yeast, and salt in a bowl.
2. Add warm water and olive oil, mixing into a dough.
3. Knead for 8-10 minutes.
4. Add olives and oregano, kneading until evenly incorporated.
5. Let the dough rise for 1 hour.
6. Shape into a loaf and place on a baking sheet.
7. Preheat the oven to 200°C (400°F) and bake for 30-35 minutes.

Cornmeal Bread

Ingredients:

- 400g all-purpose flour
- 100g cornmeal
- 10g salt
- 7g instant yeast
- 350ml warm water
- 2 tbsp olive oil

Instructions:

1. Combine flour, cornmeal, salt, and yeast in a bowl.
2. Add warm water and olive oil, mixing into a dough.
3. Knead for 8-10 minutes.
4. Let the dough rise for 1 hour.
5. Shape into a loaf and let it rise for another 30 minutes.
6. Preheat the oven to 200°C (400°F) and bake for 30-35 minutes.

Pretzel Buns

Ingredients:

- 500g all-purpose flour
- 10g salt
- 7g instant yeast
- 350ml warm water
- 30g sugar
- 2 tbsp butter
- 1 egg (for egg wash)
- Baking soda (for boiling)

Instructions:

1. Combine flour, salt, yeast, and sugar in a bowl.
2. Add warm water and butter, mixing into a dough.
3. Knead for 8-10 minutes.
4. Let the dough rise for 1 hour.
5. Preheat the oven to 200°C (400°F).
6. Shape the dough into buns and boil each in a solution of water and baking soda for 30 seconds.
7. Place the buns on a baking sheet, brush with egg wash, and bake for 15-20 minutes until golden.

Scandinavian Rye Bread

Ingredients:

- 300g rye flour
- 200g all-purpose flour
- 10g salt
- 7g instant yeast
- 350ml warm water
- 1 tbsp caraway seeds

Instructions:

1. Mix rye flour, all-purpose flour, salt, yeast, and caraway seeds in a bowl.
2. Add warm water and mix into a dough.
3. Knead for 8-10 minutes.
4. Let the dough rise for 1-2 hours.
5. Shape into a loaf and place it on a greased pan.
6. Preheat the oven to 180°C (350°F) and bake for 30-35 minutes.

www.ingramcontent.com/pod-product-compliance
Lightning Source LLC
LaVergne TN
LVHW081332060526
838201LV00055B/2588